THE ART OF MARJORIE S

ELEGANT ELEPHANTS

ADULT COLORING BOOK

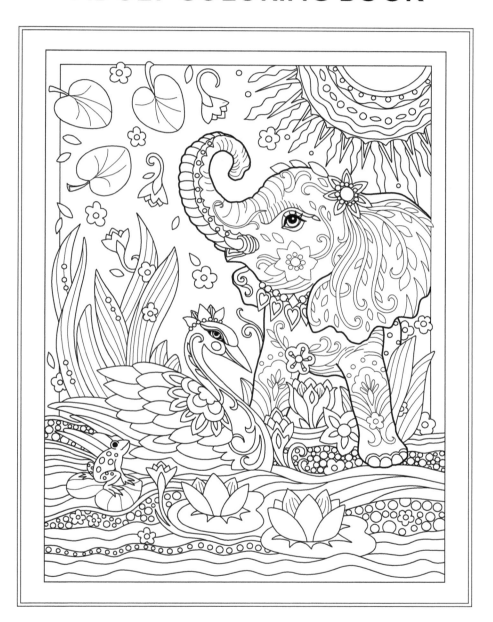

MARJORIE SARNAT

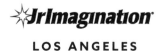

JrImagination

LOS ANGELES

The Art of Marjorie Sarnat
Elegant Elephants Adult Coloring Book

Author and Illustrator: Marjorie Sarnat
Book Design and Production: Marty Safir

Published by

Jr Imagination®
www.jrimagination.com
www.marjoriesarnat.com

ISBN: 978-0-9893189-8-3

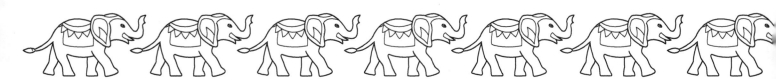

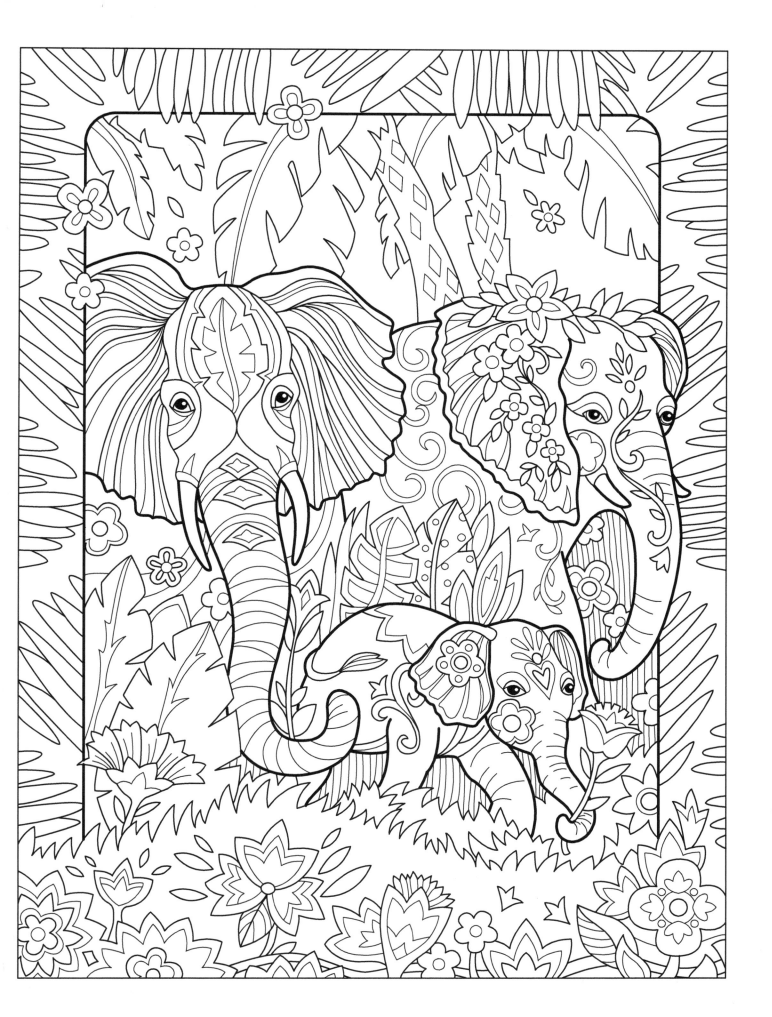

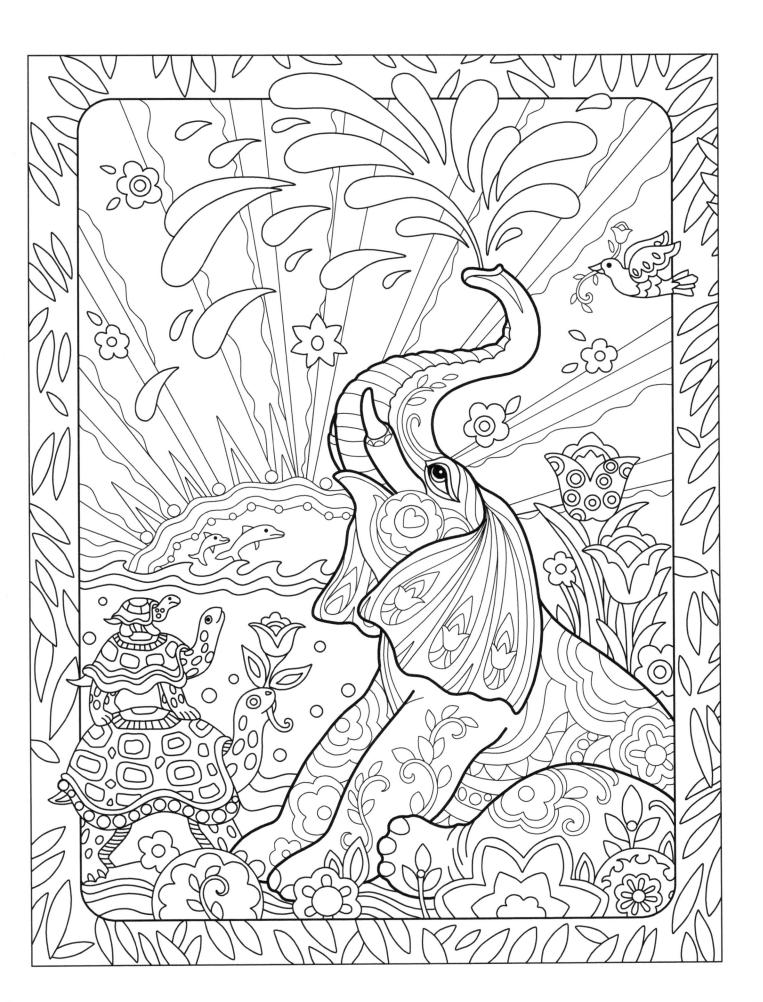

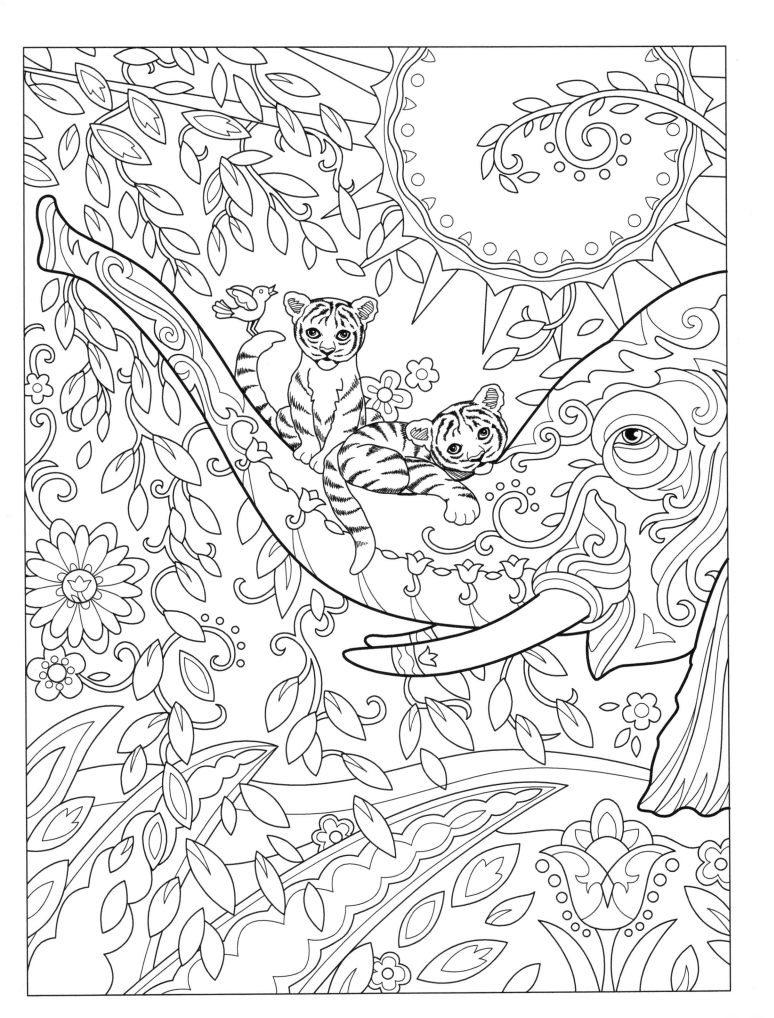

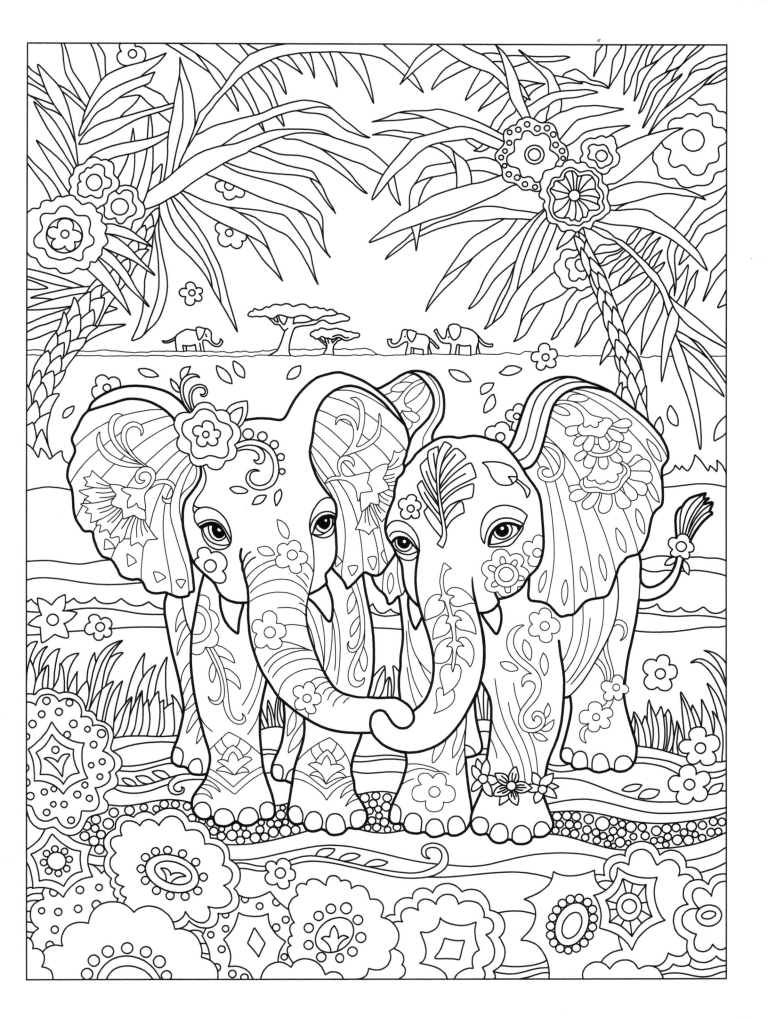

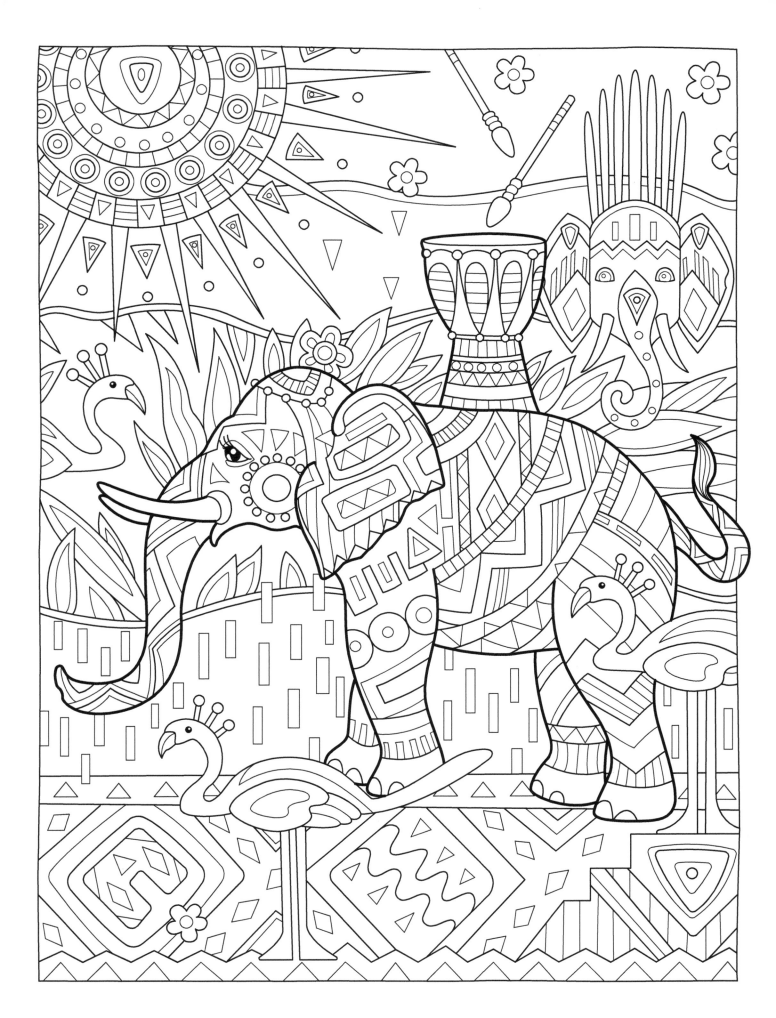

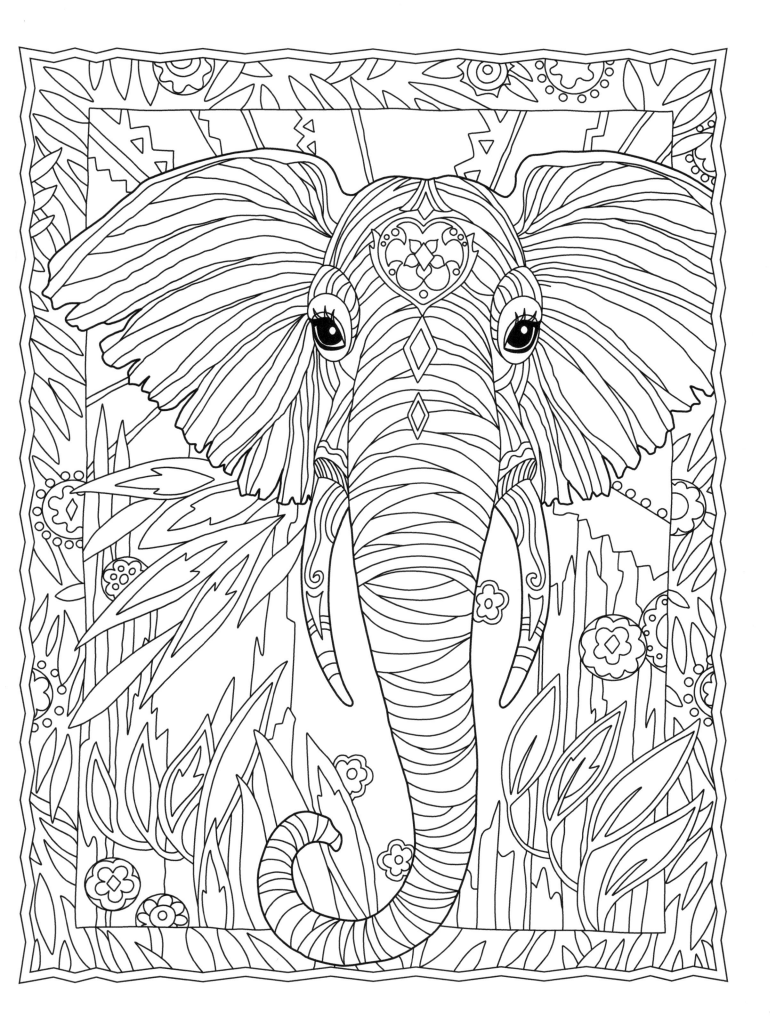

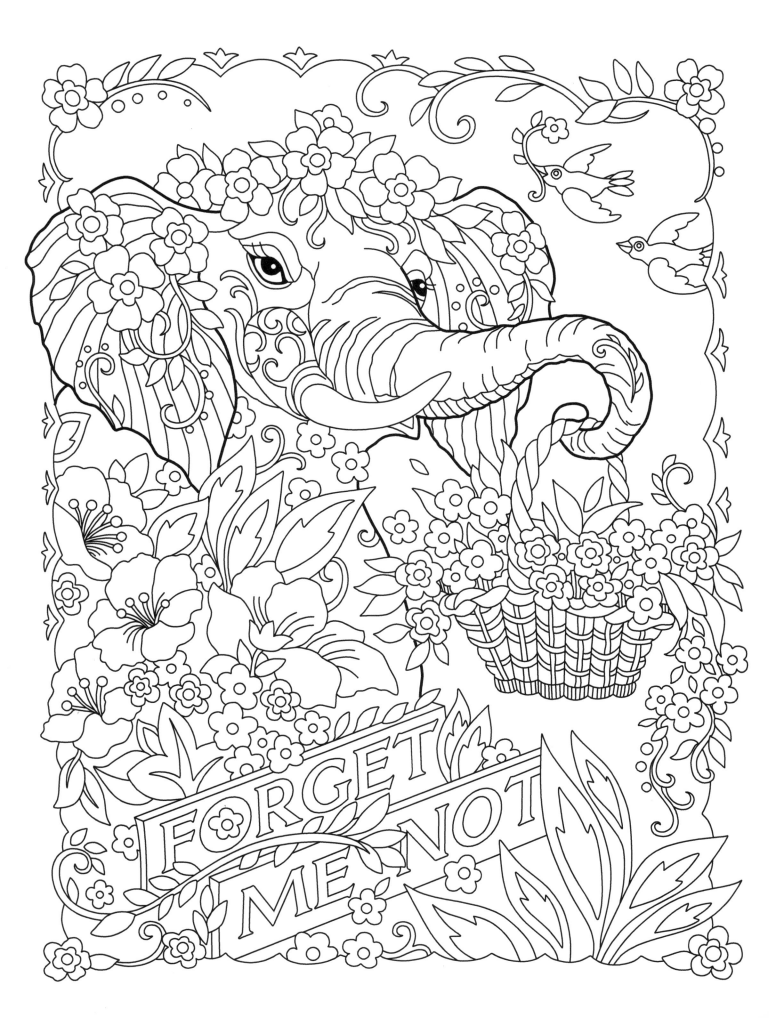

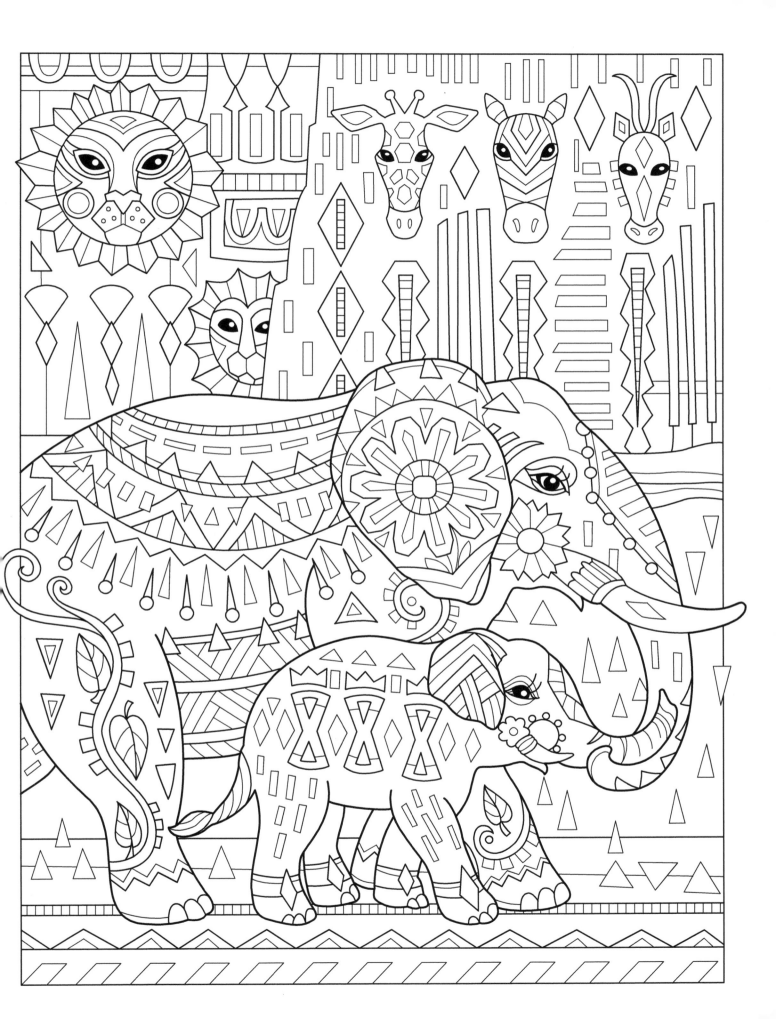

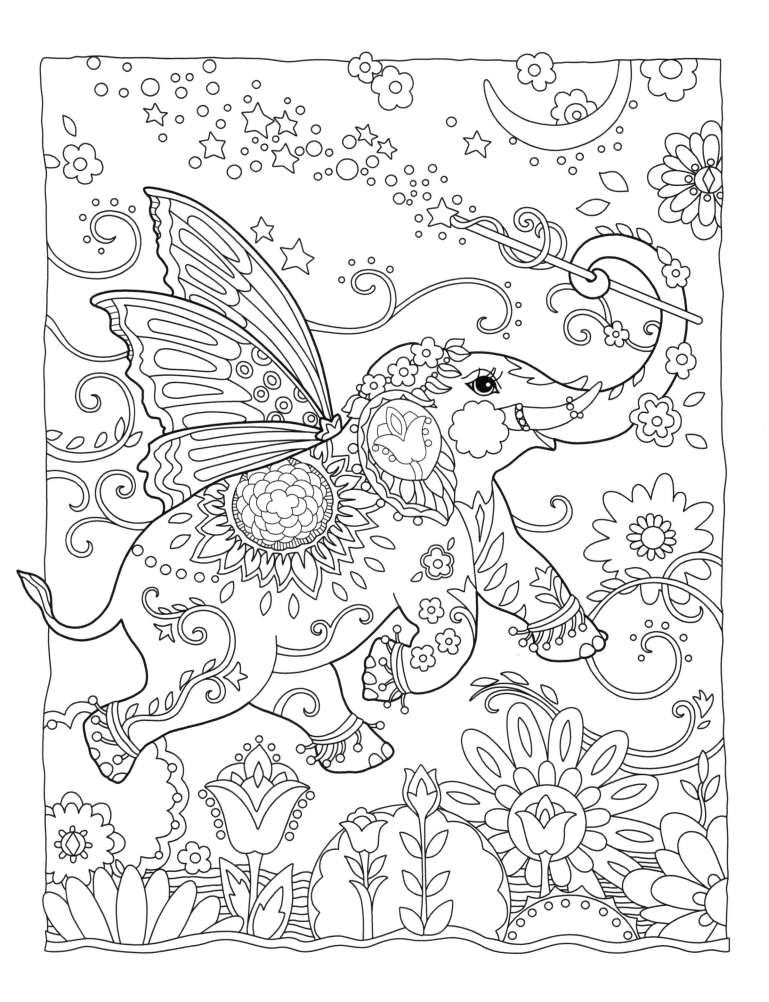

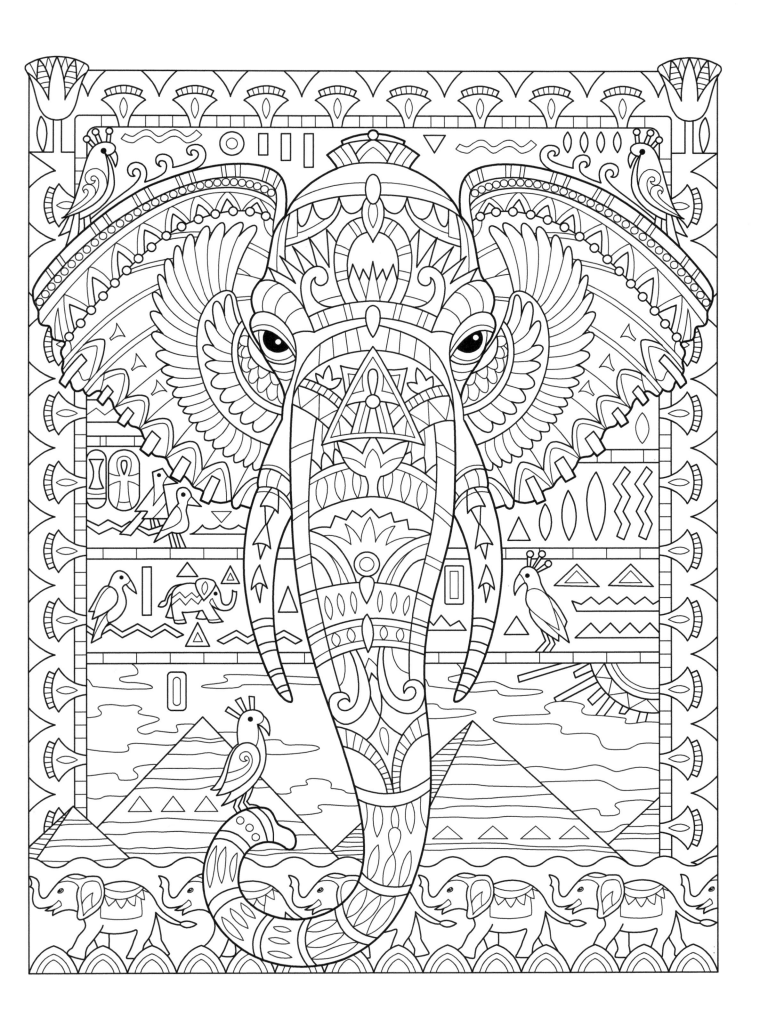

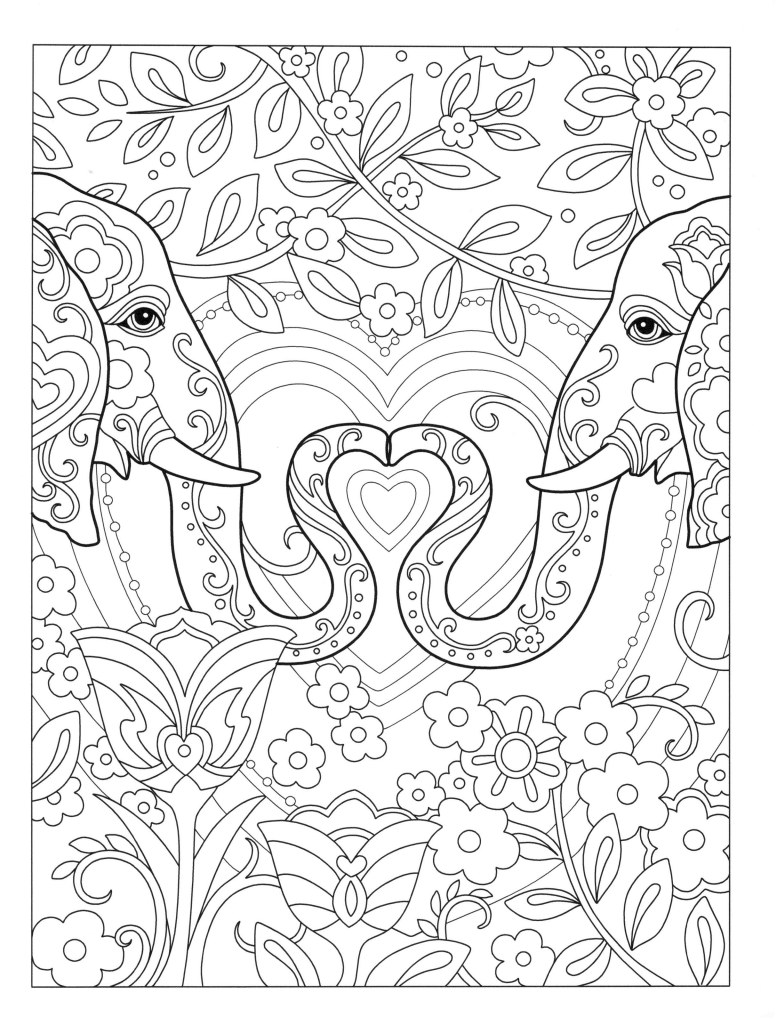

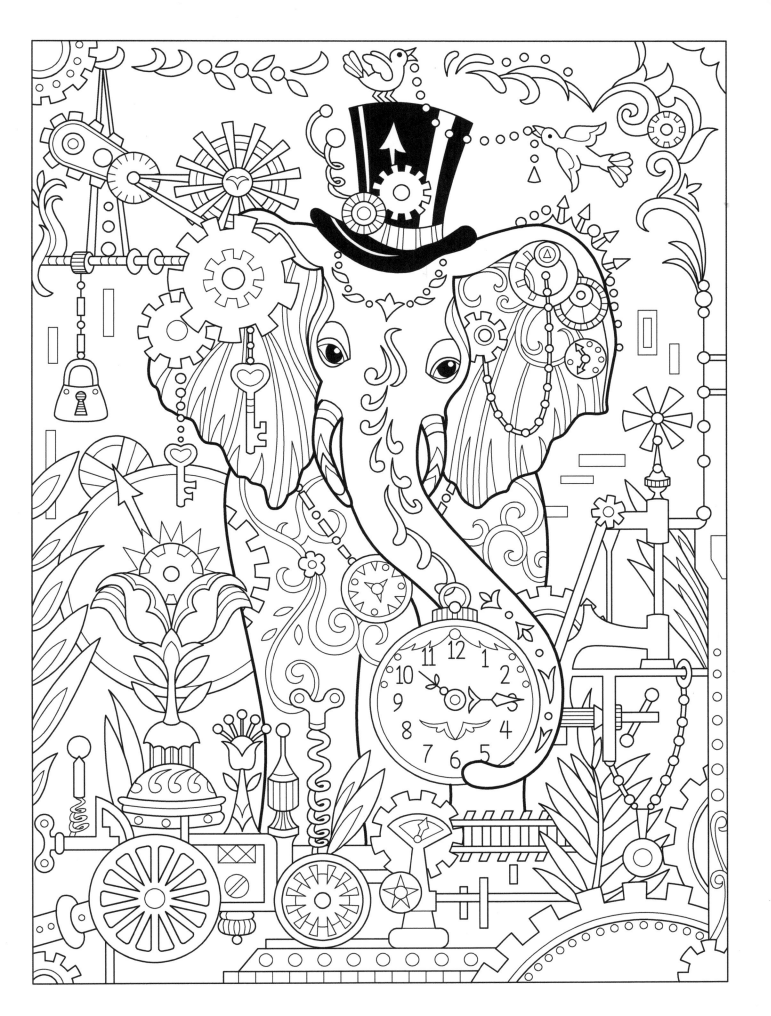

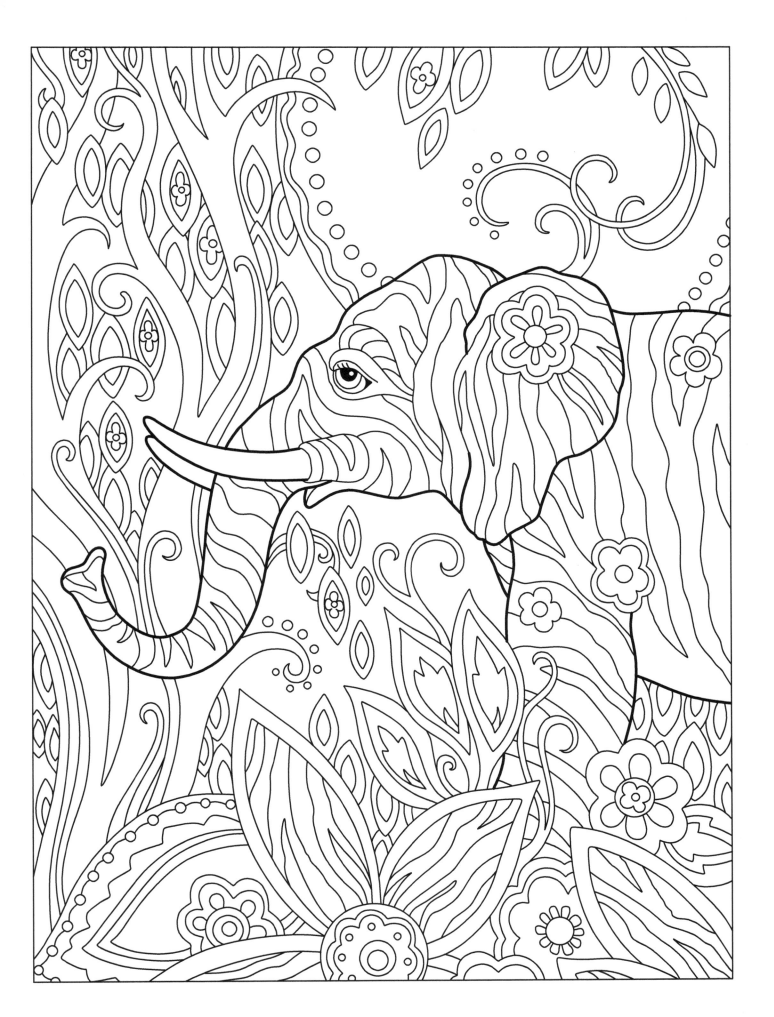

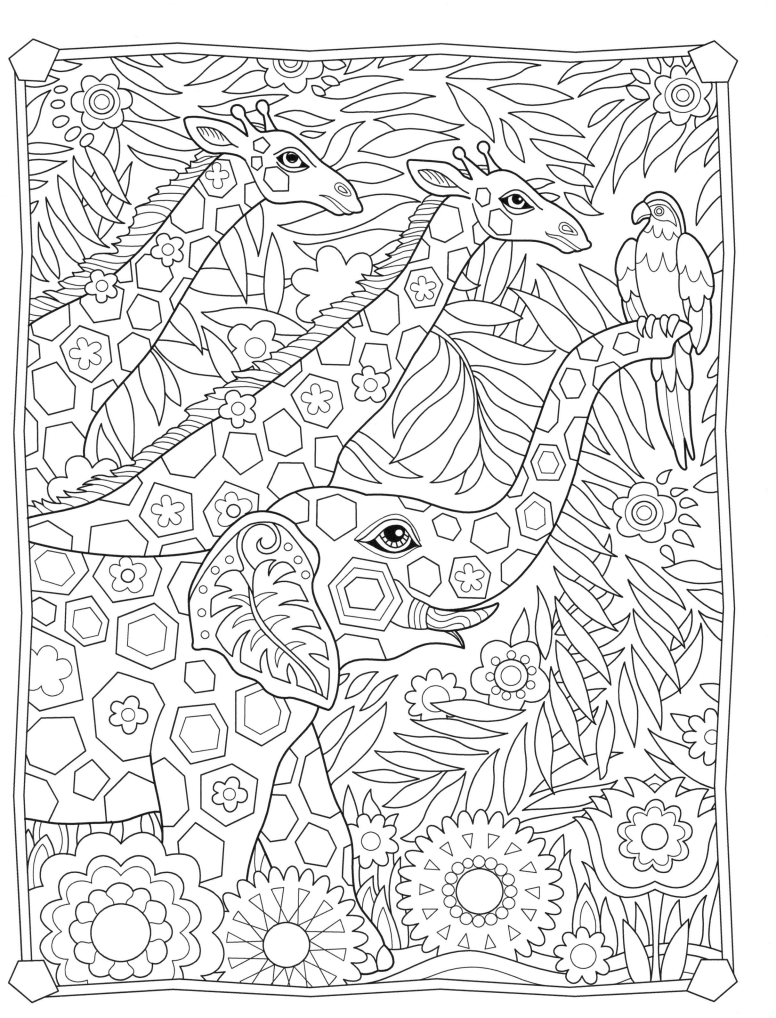

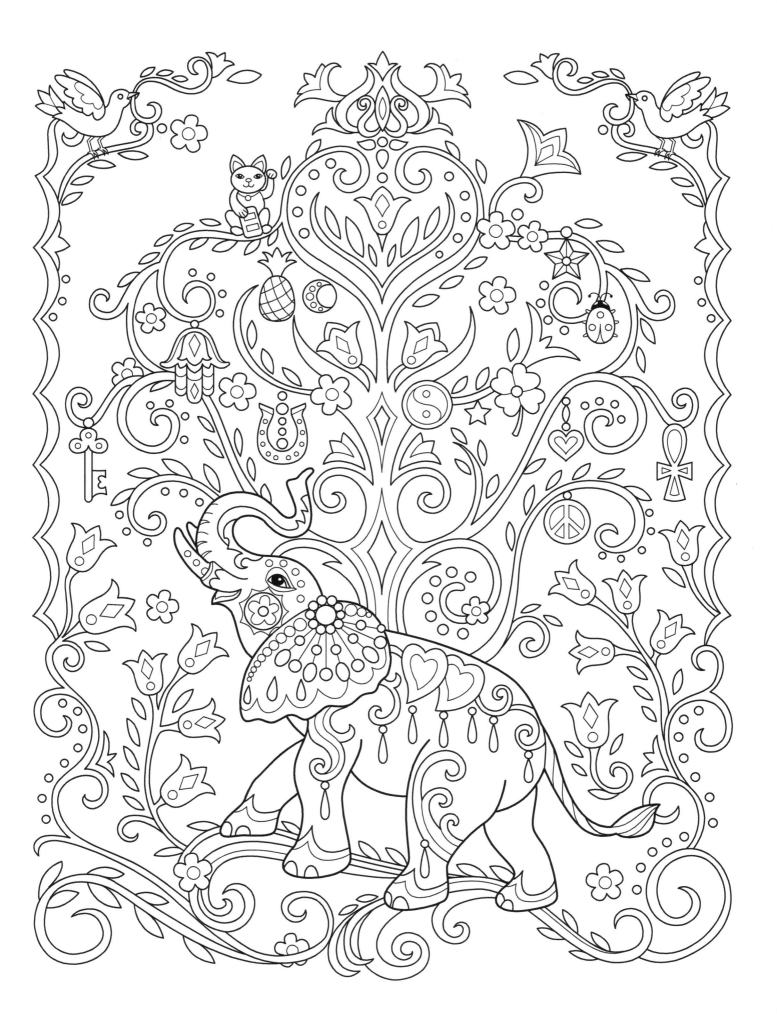

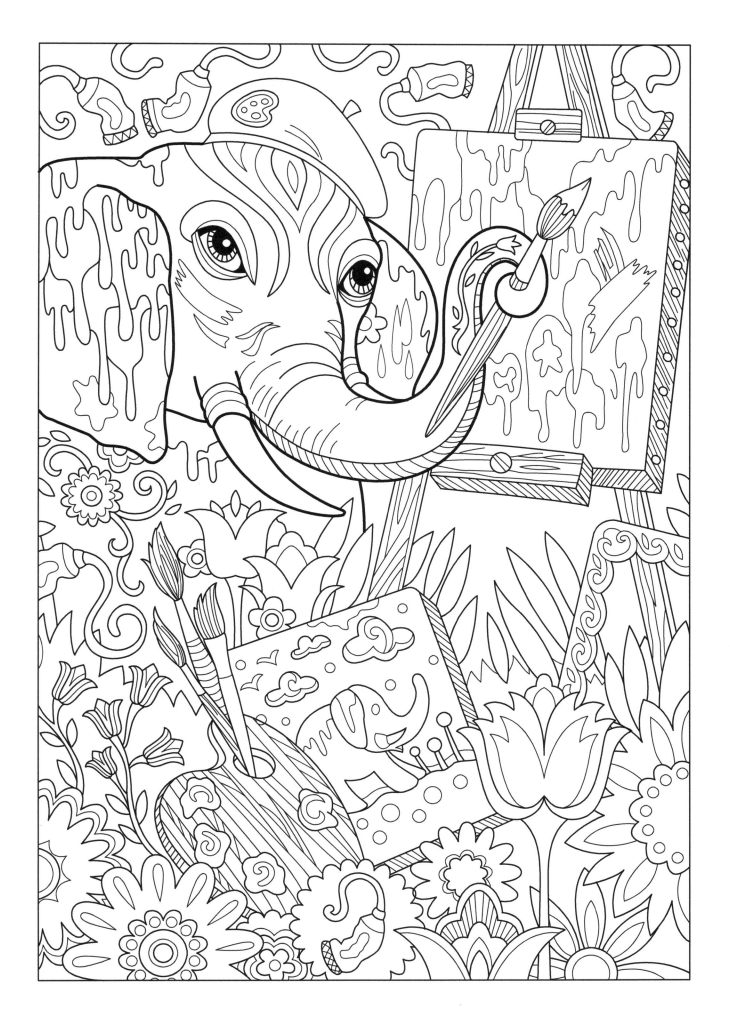

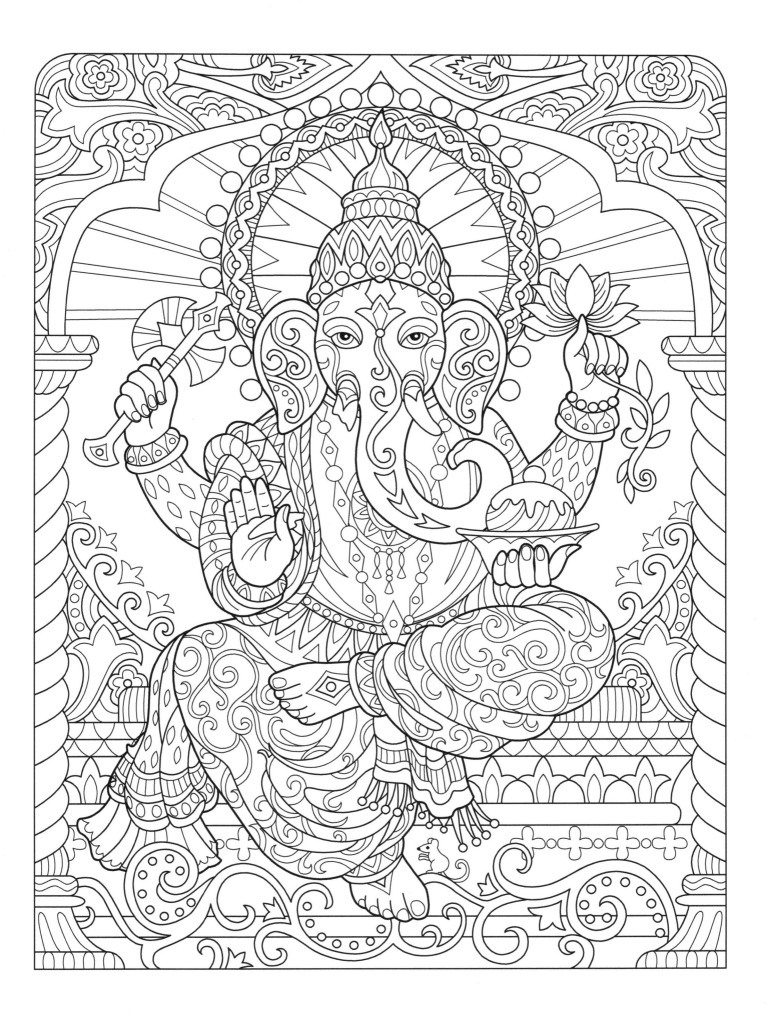

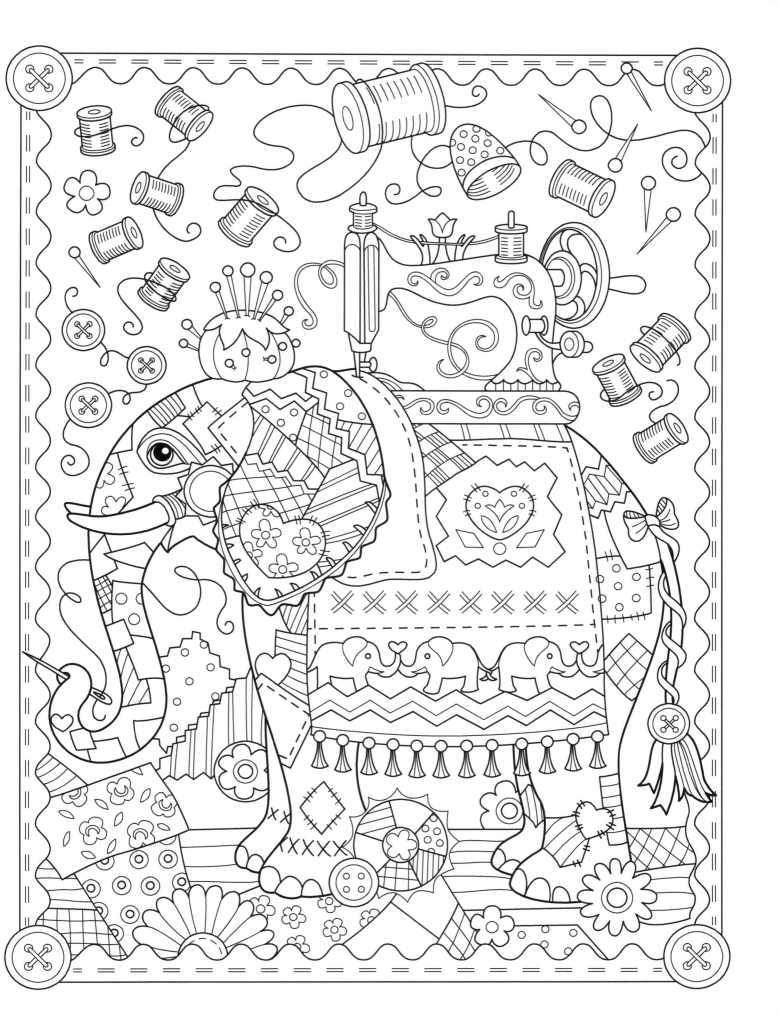

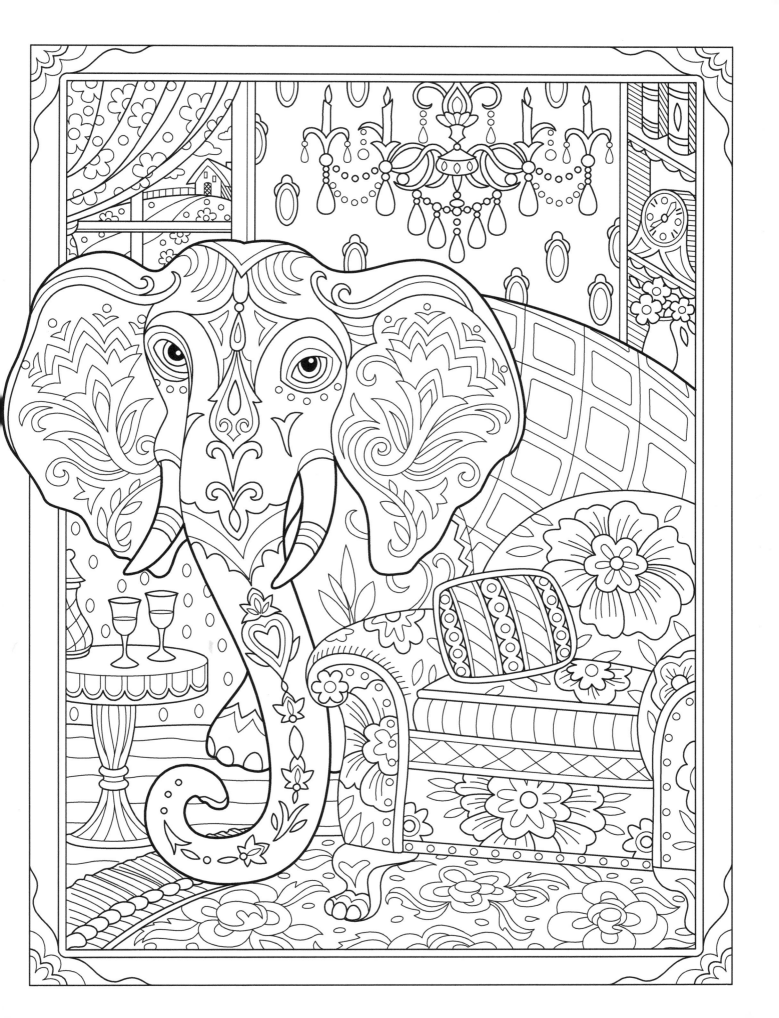

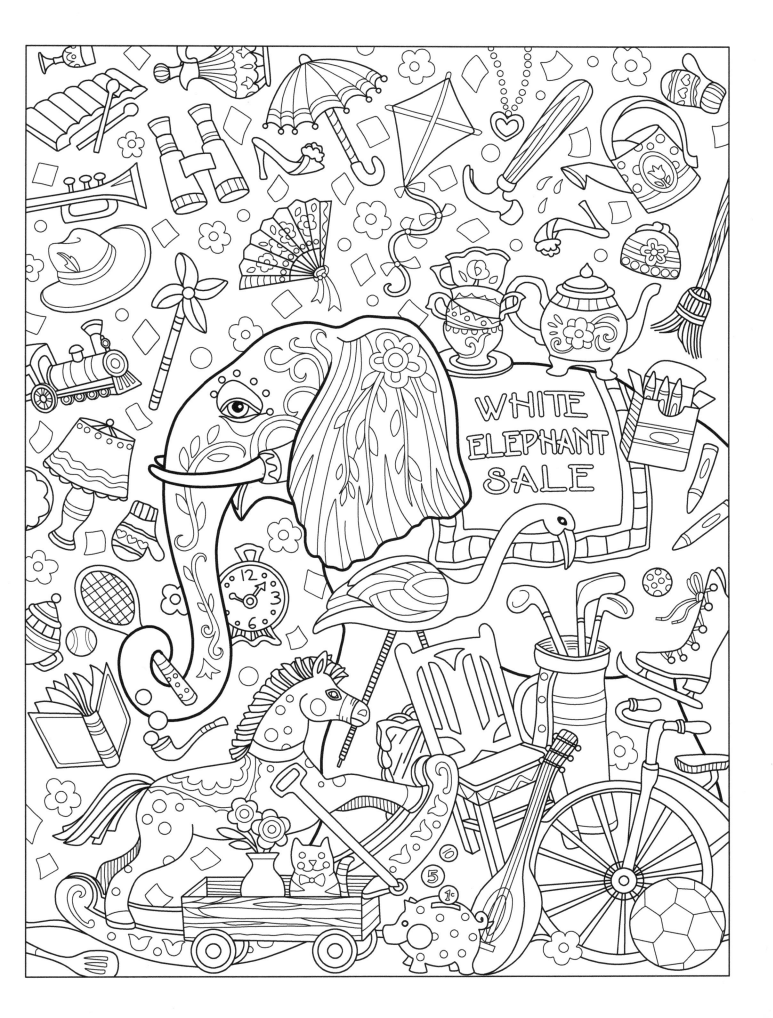

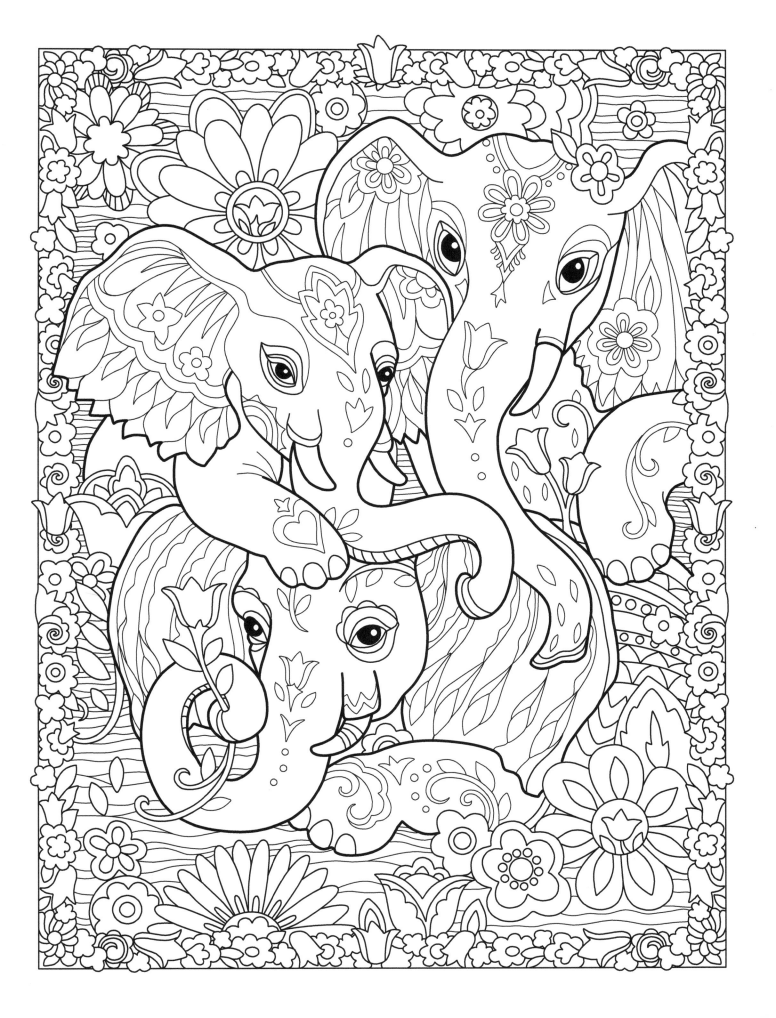

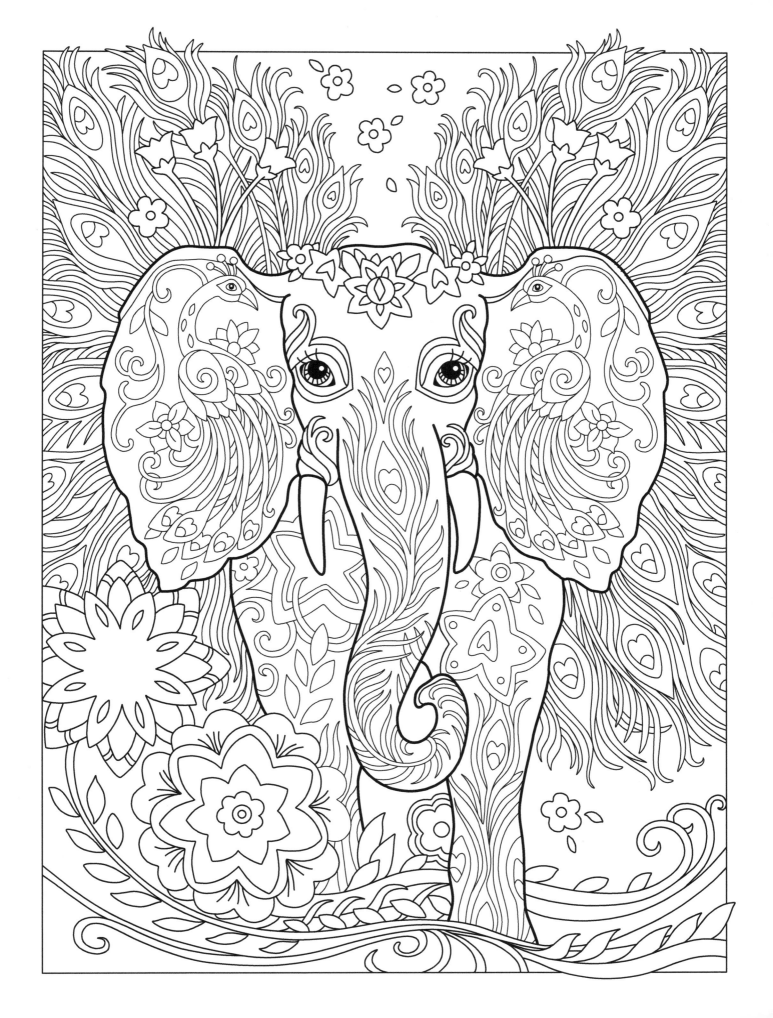

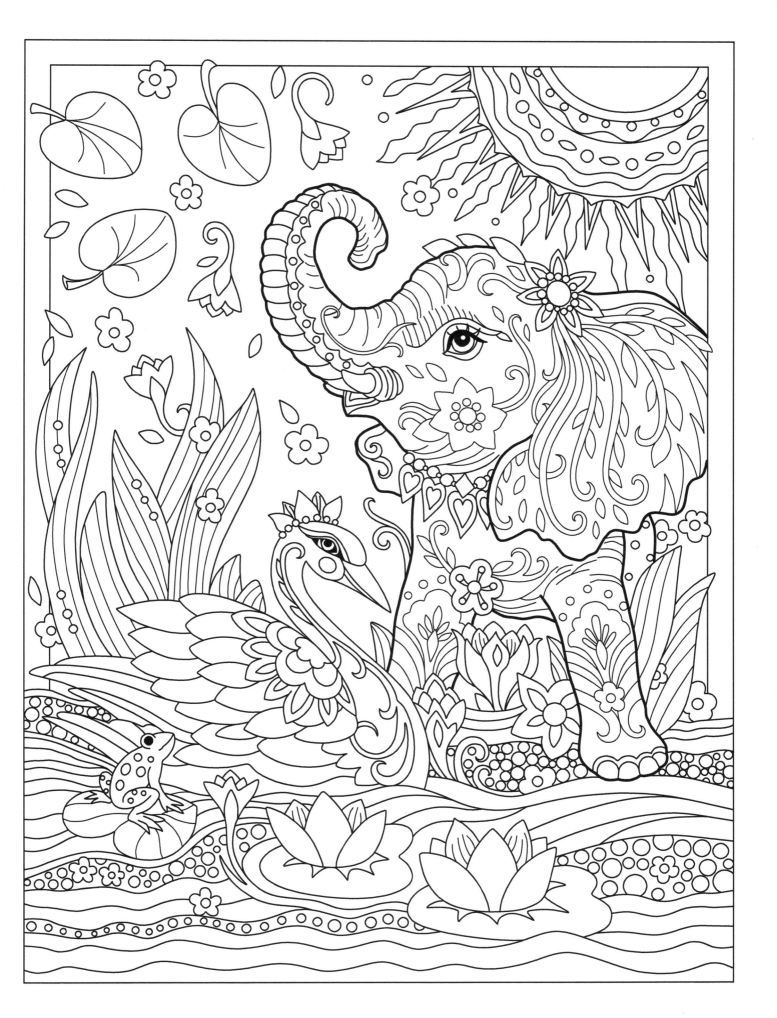

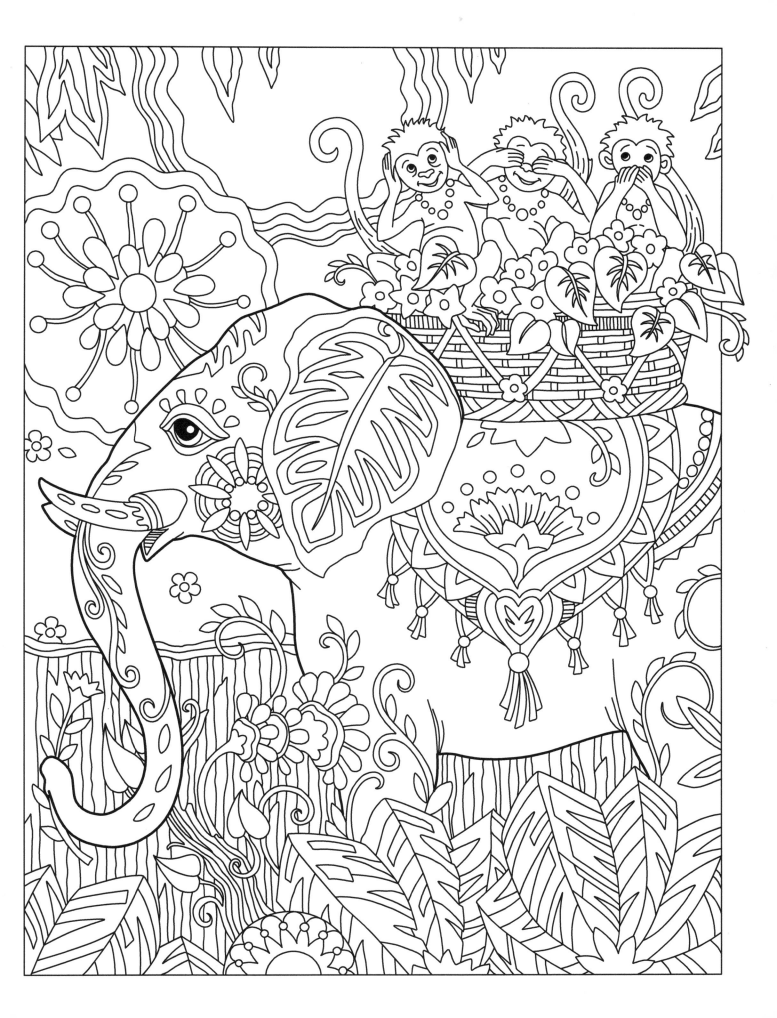

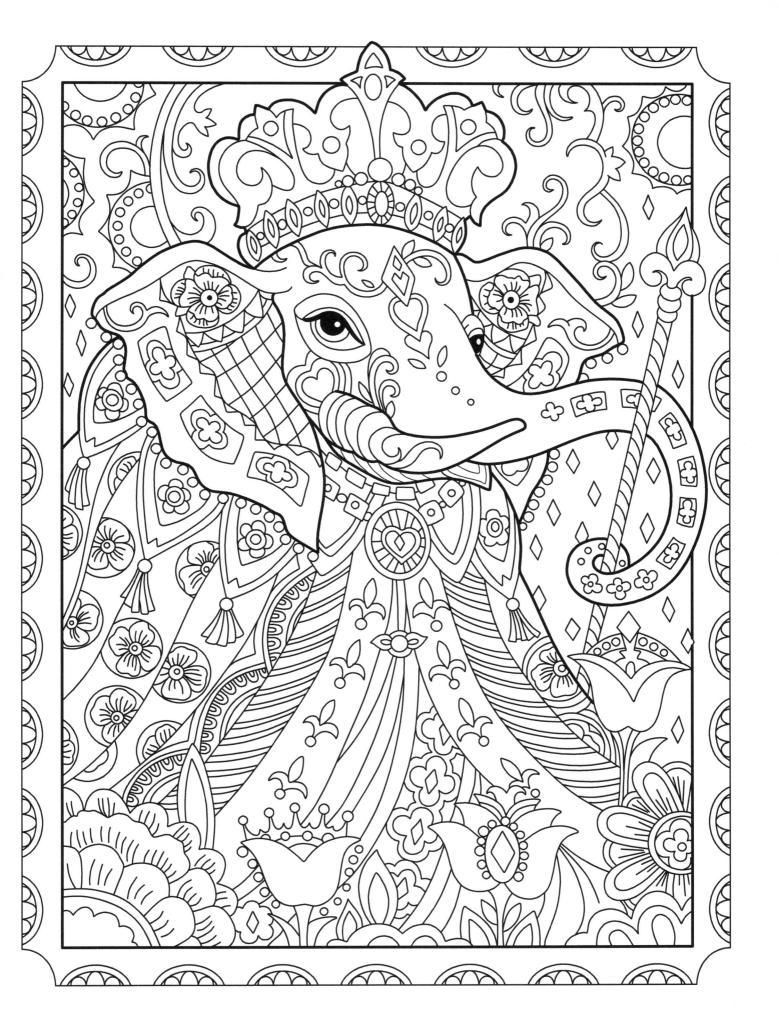

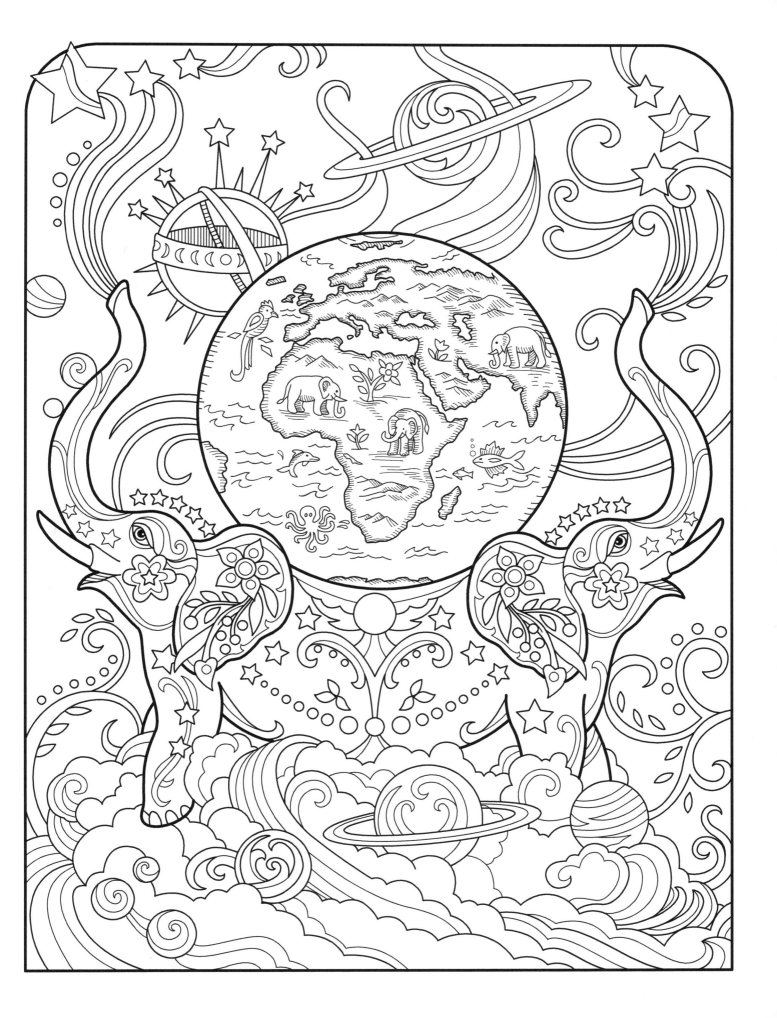

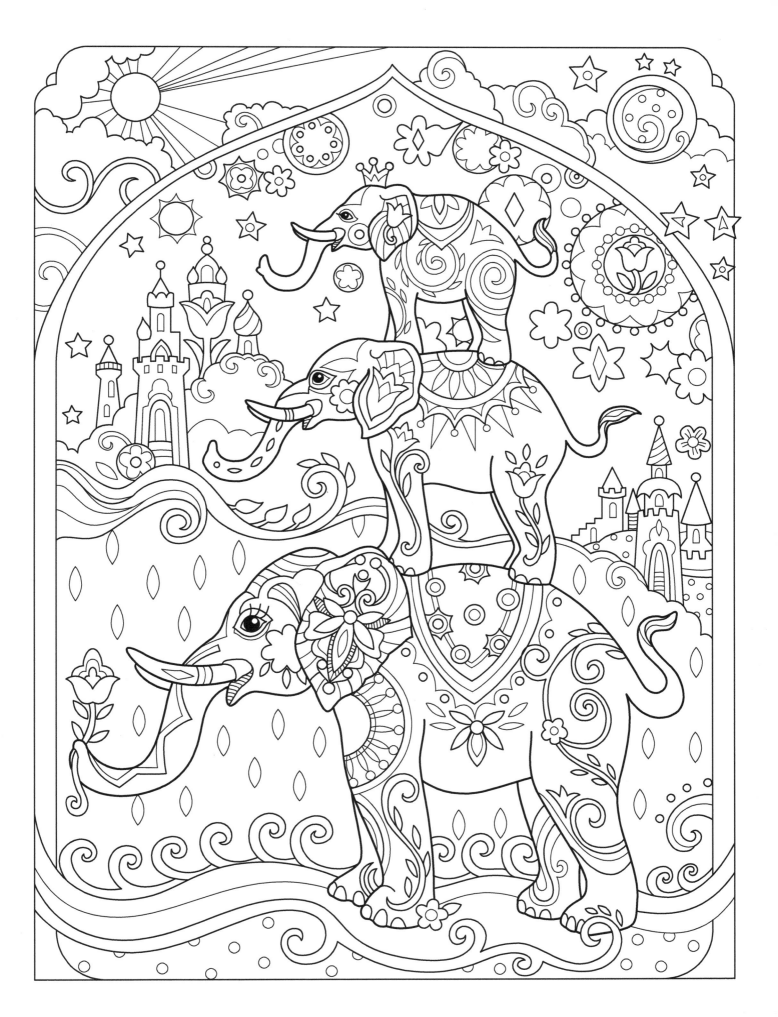

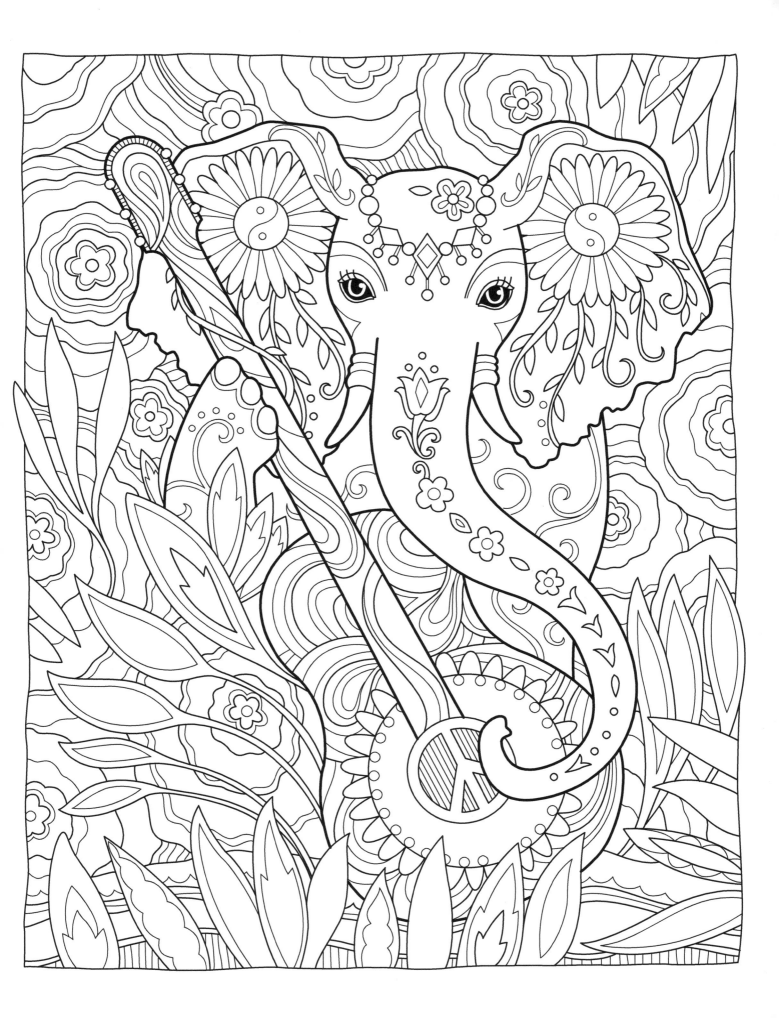

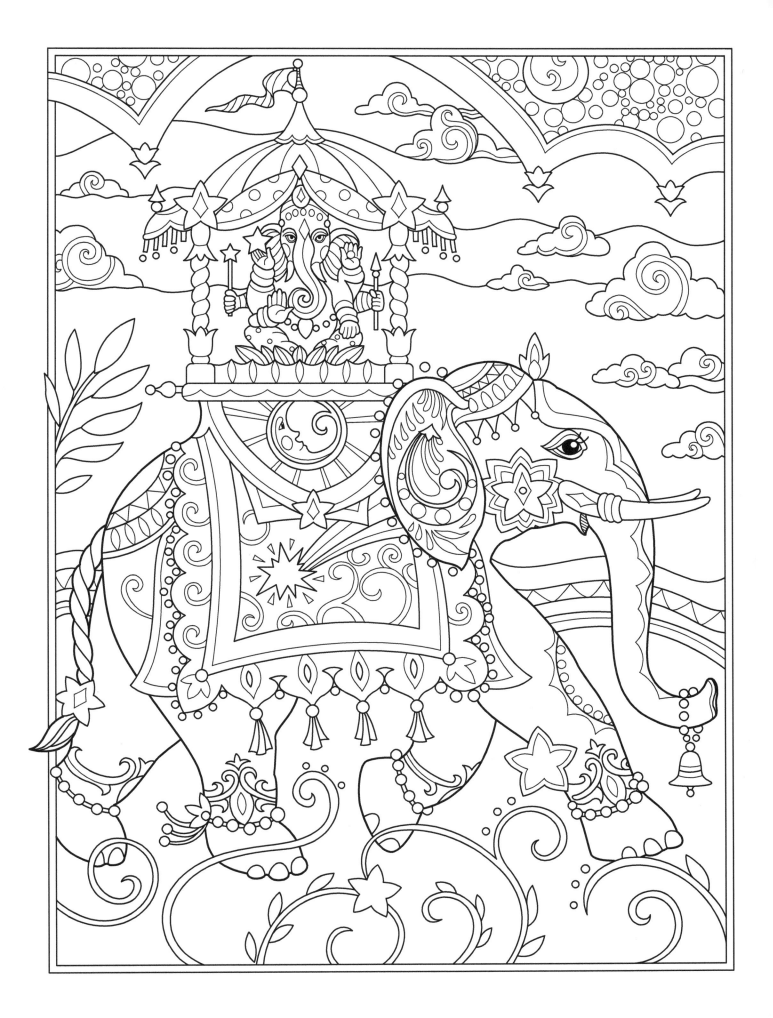

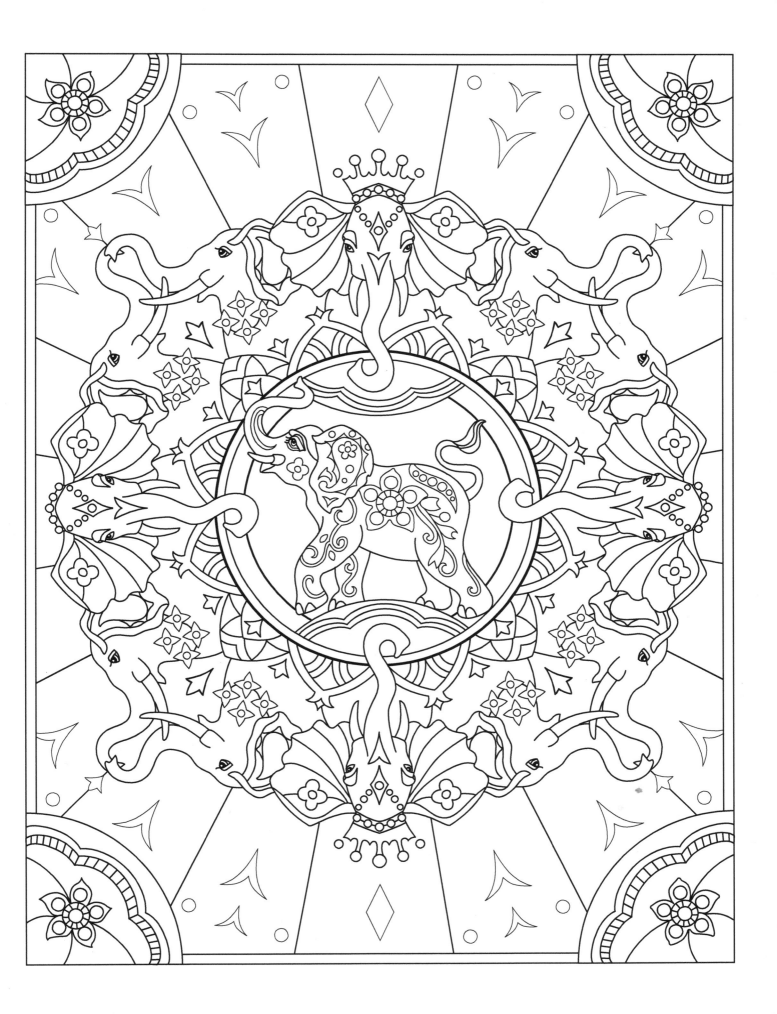

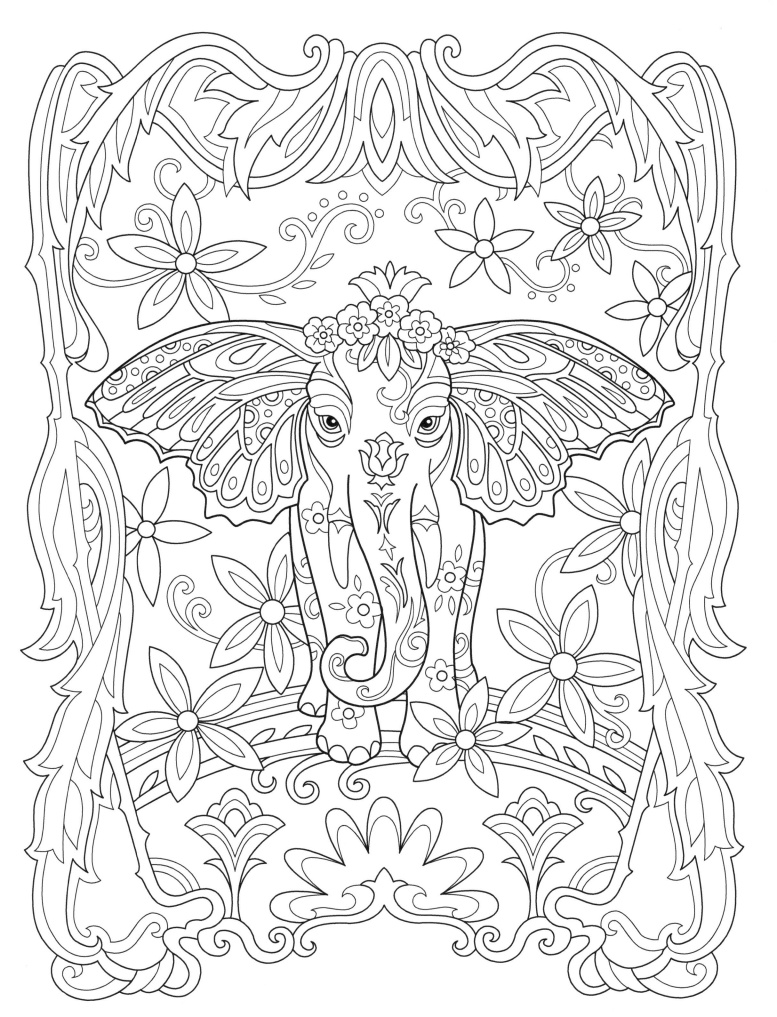

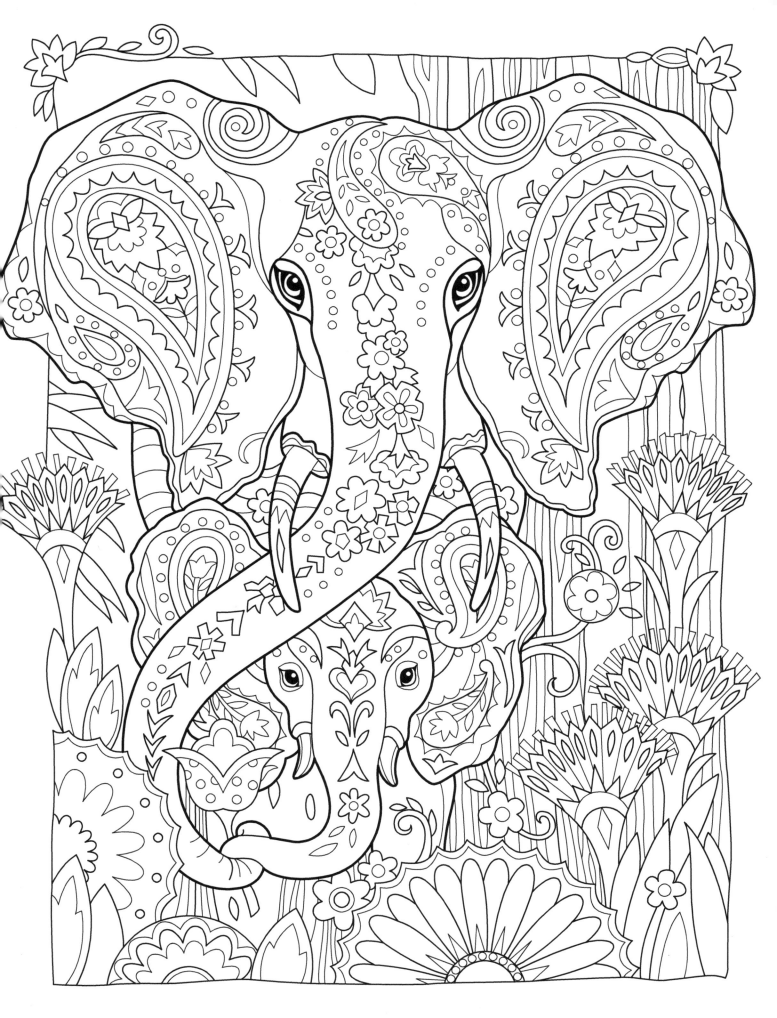

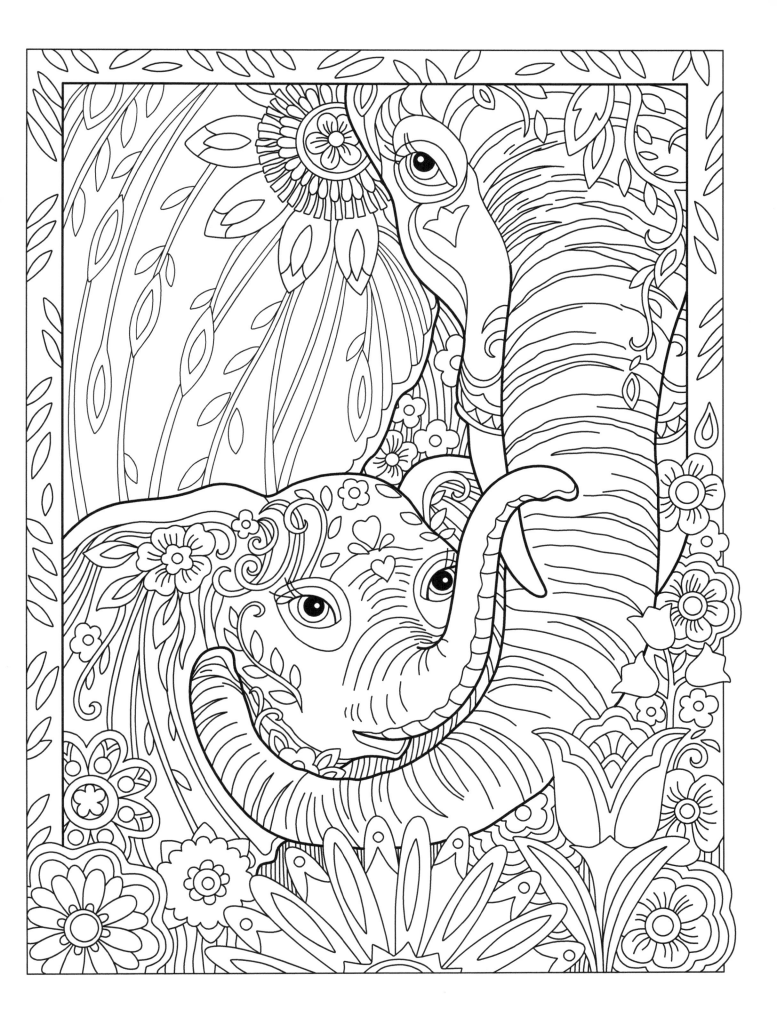

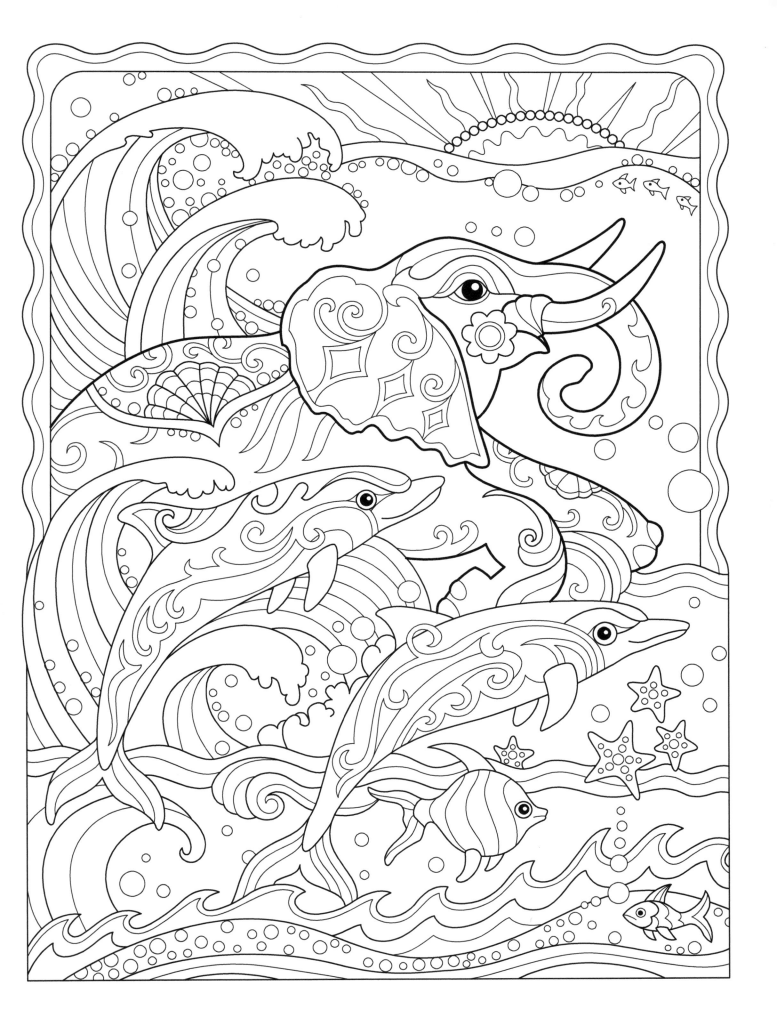

About the Author

Marjorie Sarnat's fanciful coloring book style evolved from her love of patterns, which she developed through an earlier career as a textile designer. Also influencing her style is her lifelong passion for collecting

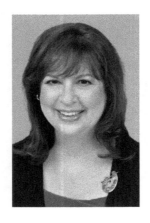

vintage illustrated books and ephemera. Her love for all things nostalgic finds its way into her coloring book imagery.

In her career, Marjorie has designed hundreds of popular collectibles and crafts that have delighted collectors throughout the world. In 2011 she co-founded Jr Imagination®, a publishing company whose books and games encourage creativity in children and adults.

Marjorie's bestsellers include *Creative Cats Coloring Book*, and *Owls Coloring Book*, together which have sold over a million copies. Her *Pampered Pets*, *Fanciful Fashions*, and *Dazzling Dogs* coloring books are earning rave reviews from new and experienced colorists alike.

Born and raised in Chicago, Marjorie is an alumna of the School of the Art Institute of Chicago and earned a BFA degree from Eastern Michigan University. Marjorie lives in Southern California with her husband, daughter, son, two funny dogs, and her extensive antique book collection.

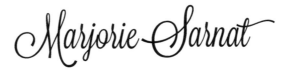

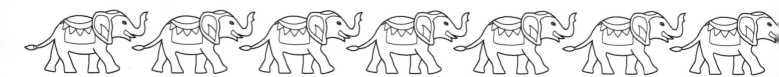

Connect with Marjorie

I enjoy being in touch with colorists and other artists, so please feel free to contact me with comments or suggestions.

MY WEBSITES
Design and Illustration   www.marjoriesarnat.com
Fine Art   www.sarnatart.com
Creative Thinking   www.jrimagination.com

MY BLOGS
Marjorie's Coloring Journal   www.marjoriesarnat.com/blog
Art Studio Secrets Blog   www.art-studio-secrets.com
Raising a Creative Genius Blog   www.jrimagination.com/blog

SOCIAL MEDIA
Twitter   @MarjorieSarnat
Facebook   www.facebook.com/marjoriesarnat (click Follow)
Amazon Author Page   amazon.com/author/marjoriesarnat

SUPPORT
Email   service@marjoriesarnat.com

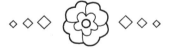

Join My Email List

Sign up to receive "For Color Lovers," at
www.marjoriesarnat.com/for-color-lovers
for notice about new releases, free coloring pages,
giveaways, tips and techniques, and more.

Also by Marjorie Sarnat

Dazzling Dogs Coloring Book

Marjorie Sarnat's Pampered Pets
New York Times Bestselling Artists' Adult Coloring Books

Marjorie Sarnat's Fanciful Fashions
New York Times Bestselling Artists' Adult Coloring Books

Creative Cats Coloring Book

Owls Coloring Book

Textile Designs Coloring Book

Fanciful Foxes Coloring Book

Creative Cats Sticker Book

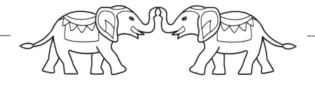

151 Uncommon and Amazing Art Studio Secrets

151 Effective and Extraordinary Art Studio Secrets

210 Imaginative Ideas for Painting

Creative Genius: How to Grow the Seeds of Creativity Within Every Child

Creativity Unhinged: 120 Games for Kids to Spark Creative Thinking

"As a coloring book artist I enjoy delighting the colorist with beautiful and detailed themes on every page. Each drawing displays a profusion of patterns and imaginative settings for the colorist to bring to life. I hope that the experience of coloring my artwork is inspiring, fun, and helps release everyday stress.

"I've received kind words and enthusiasm about my work from colorists throughout the world. Thank you from the bottom of my heart. I'm grateful for your support."

– MARJORIE SARNAT

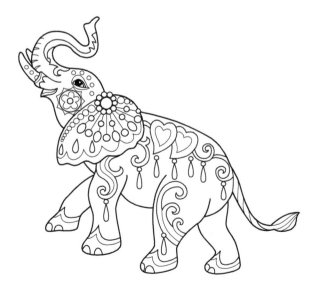

CPSIA information can be obtained
at www.ICGtesting.com
Printed in the USA
BVHW092138261221
624757BV00004B/208